SCHAUM POPULAR PIANO PIECES
A-THE RED BOOK

P9-DVZ-060

SHEET MUSIC

Project Manager: Gail Lew

Cover Art: Martha Ramirez

© 1987 BELWIN-MILLS PUBLISHING CORP. (ASCAP)
This edition © 2000 BELWIN-MILLS PUBLISHING CORP. (ASCAP)
All Rights Administered by WARNER BROS. PUBLICATIONS U.S. INC.
All Rights Reserved including Public Performance for Profit

Somewhere, My Love
(Lara's Theme from "Doctor Zhivago")

Words by PAUL FRANCIS WEBSTER

Music by MAURICE JARRE
Arr. by John W. Schaum, A.S.C.A.P.

Moderato

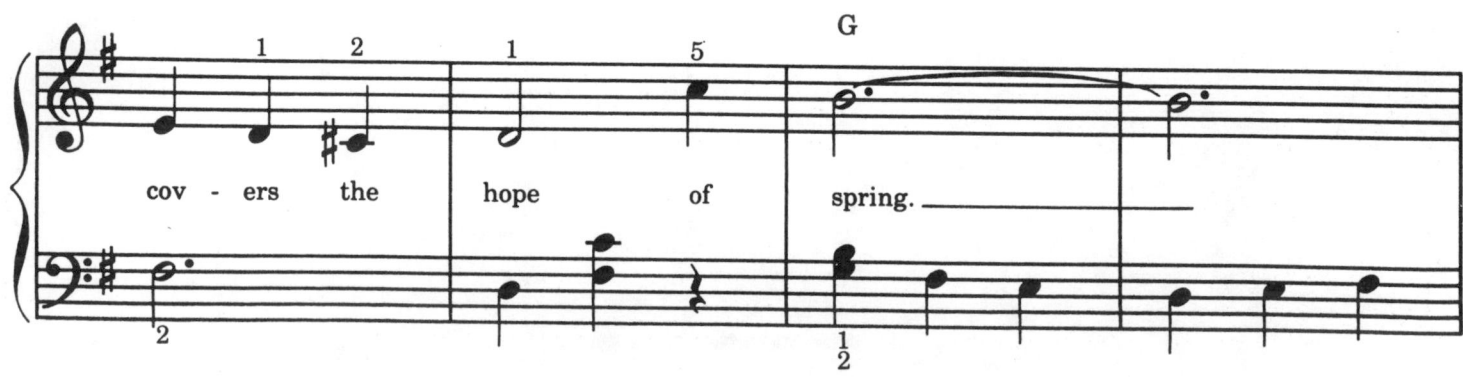

EL03368

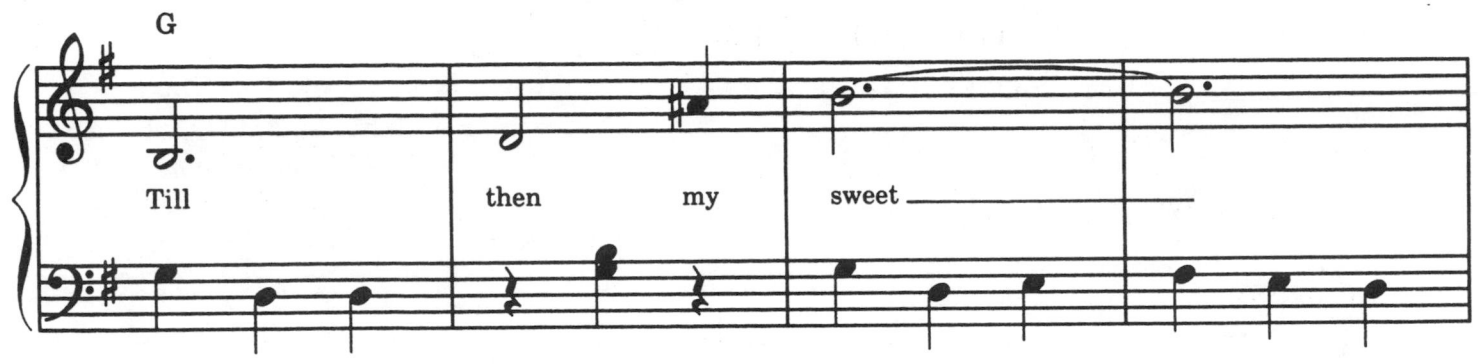

Till then my sweet

think of me now and then,

God - speed my love

till you are mine a - gain.

Happiness Is

Words and Music by
PAUL PARNES and PAUL EVANS
Arr. by Wesley Schaum

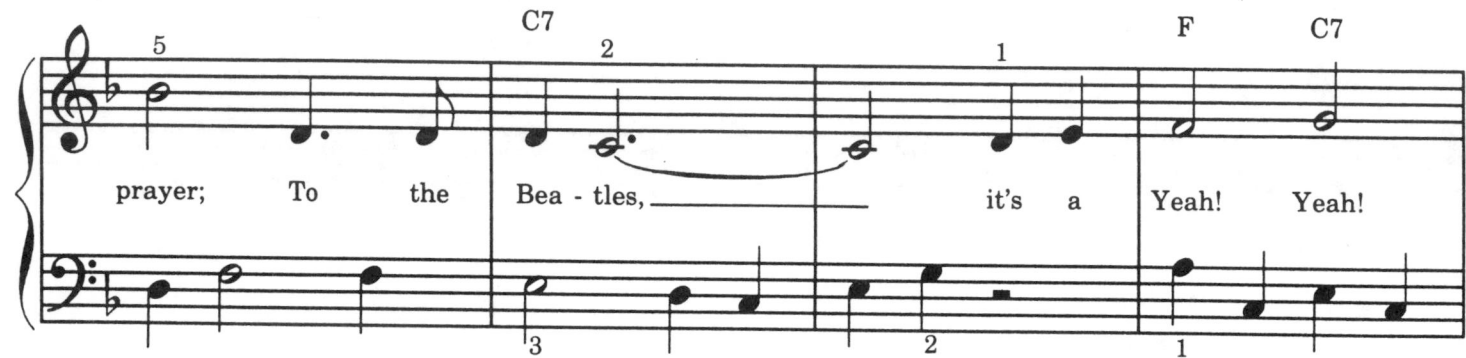

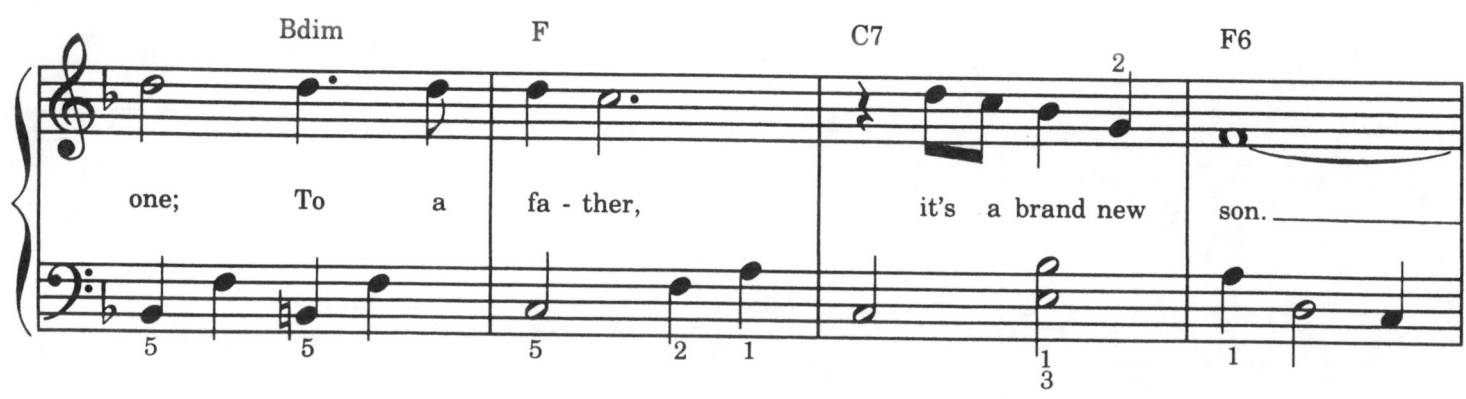

EL03368

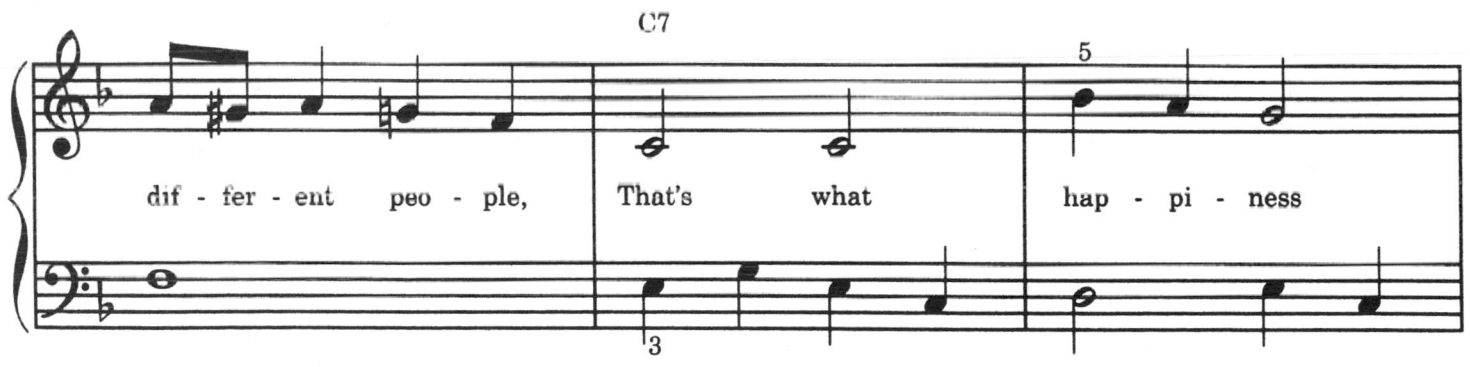

As Sung In The Paramount Picture "BREAKFAST AT TIFFANY'S"

Moon River

Words by JOHNNY MERCER

Music by HENRY MANCINI

Arr. by Wesley Schaum

Sung by GENE KELLY in "SINGIN' IN THE RAIN" (MGM 1952)

Singin' In The Rain

Lyric by
ARTHUR FREED

Music by
NACIO HERB BROWN
Arr. by Wesley Schaum

EL03368

love. Let the storm - y clouds chase Ev - 'ry - one from the

place, Come on with the rain, I've a smile on my

face. I'll walk down the lane with a hap - py re -

frain, And sing - in' just sing - in' in the rain. _____

From The Paramount Picture "THE STERILE CUCKOO"

Come Saturday Morning

Words by
DORY PREVIN

Music by
FRED KARLIN
Arr. by John W. Schaum, A.S.C.A.P.

trav - el for miles in our Sat - ur - day smiles. _____

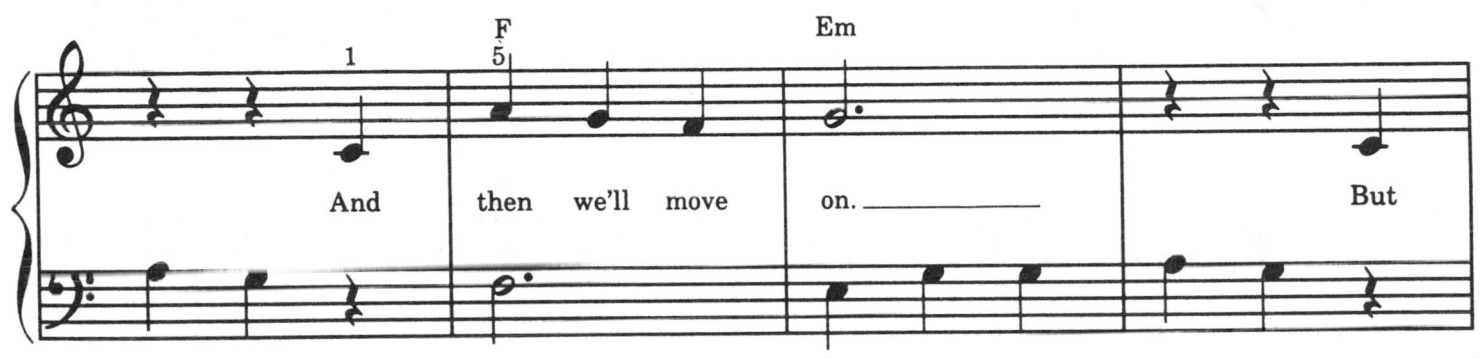

And then we'll move on. _____ But

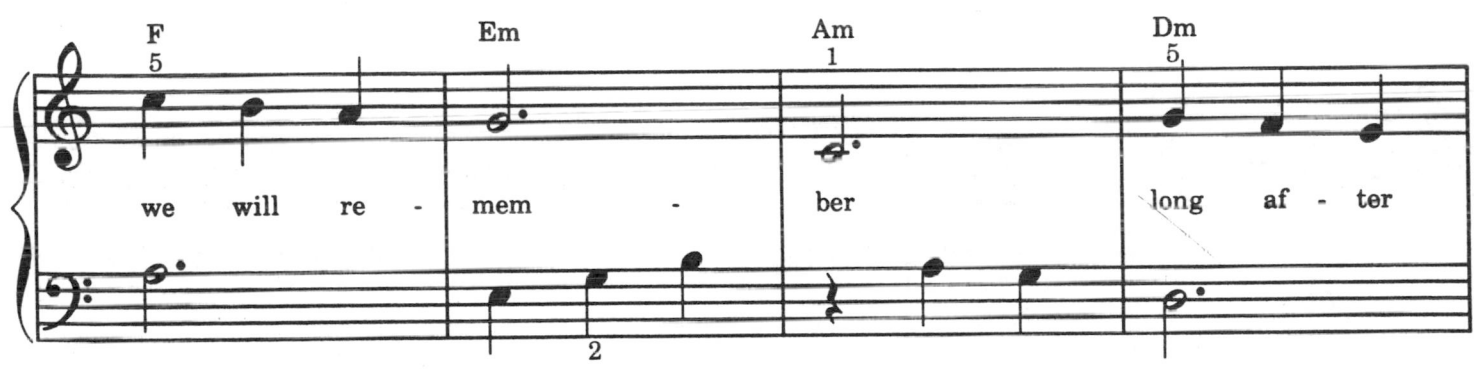

we will re - mem - ber long af - ter

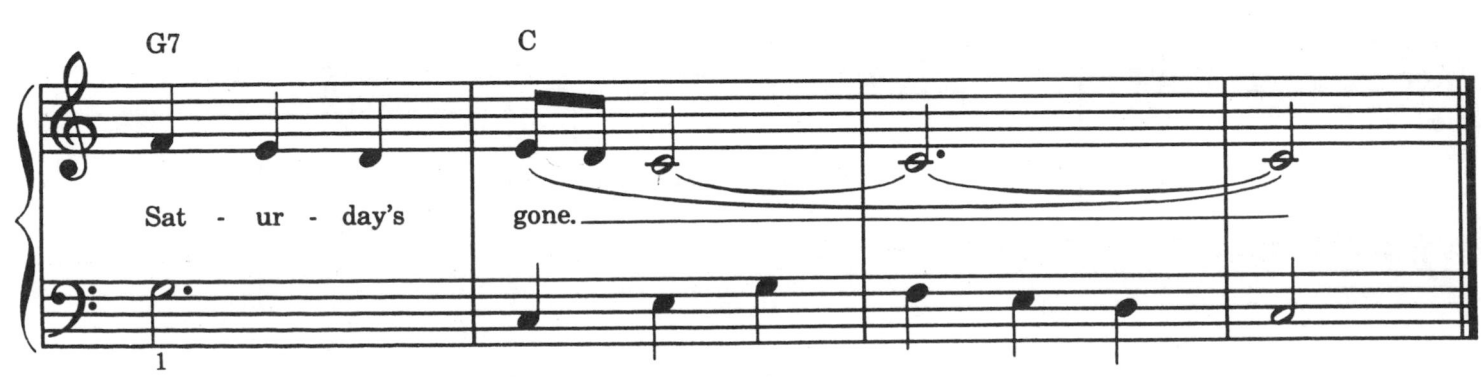

Sat - ur - day's gone. _____

You're The Inspiration

Words and Music by
PETER CETERA and
DAVID FOSTER
Arr. by Wesley Schaum

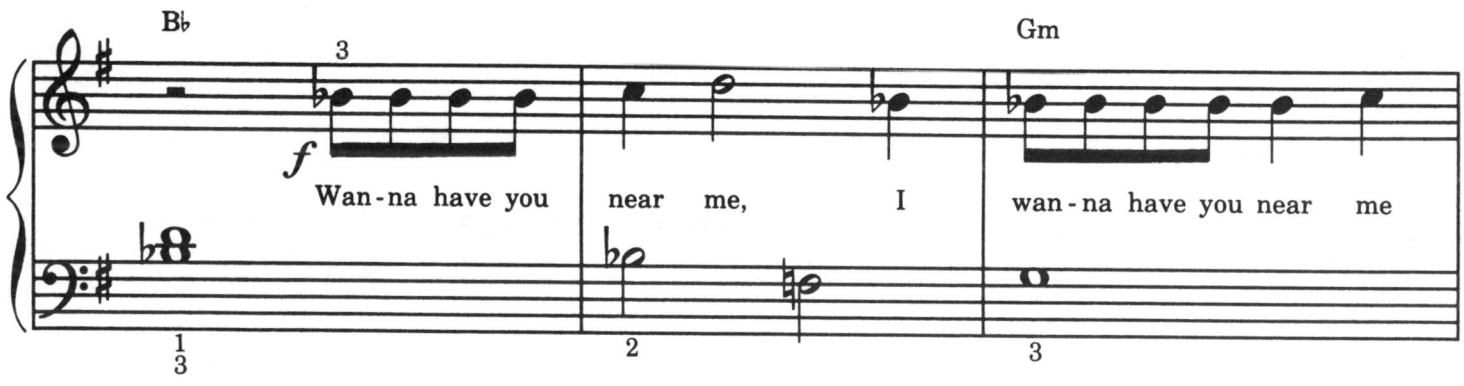

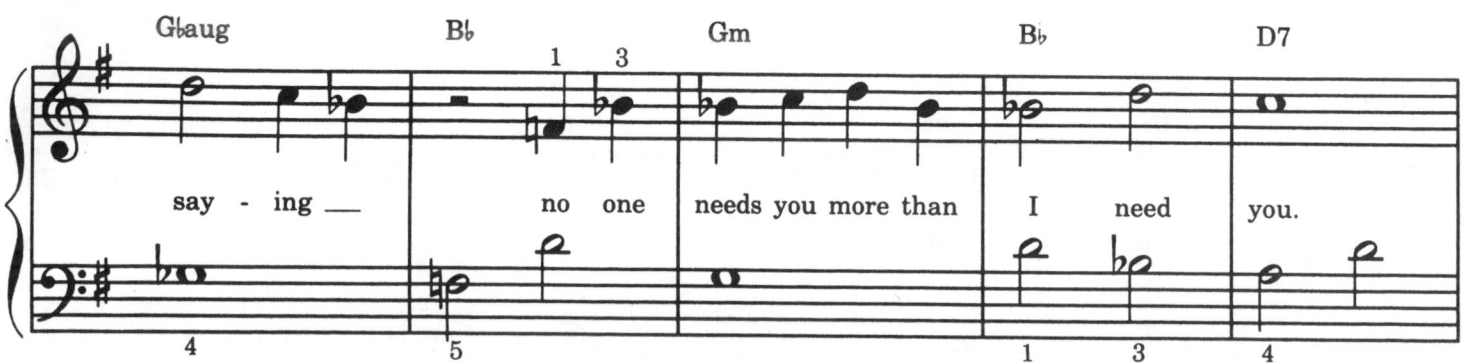

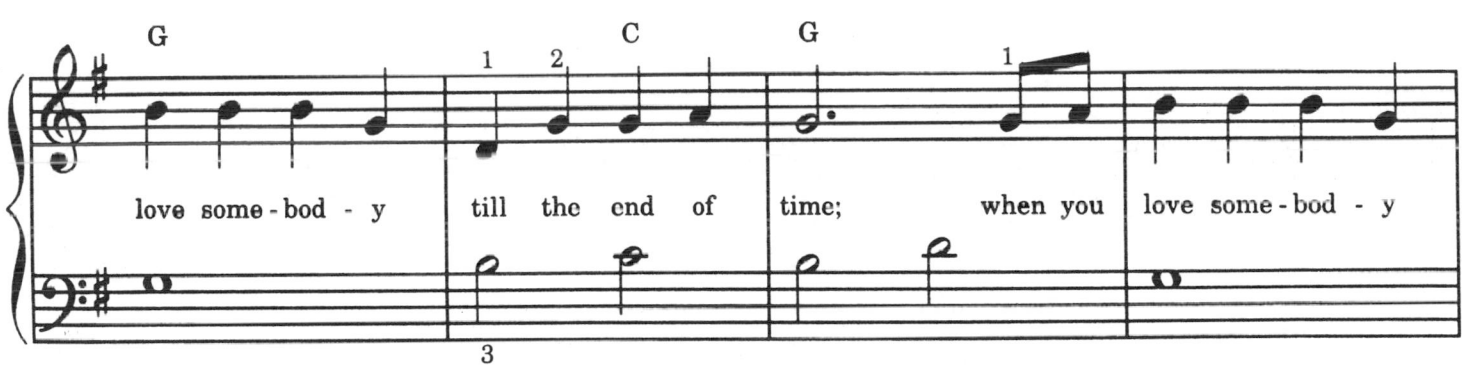

Tonight I Celebrate My Love

Words and Music by
MICHAEL MASSER and
GERRY GOFFIN
Arr. by Wesley Schaum

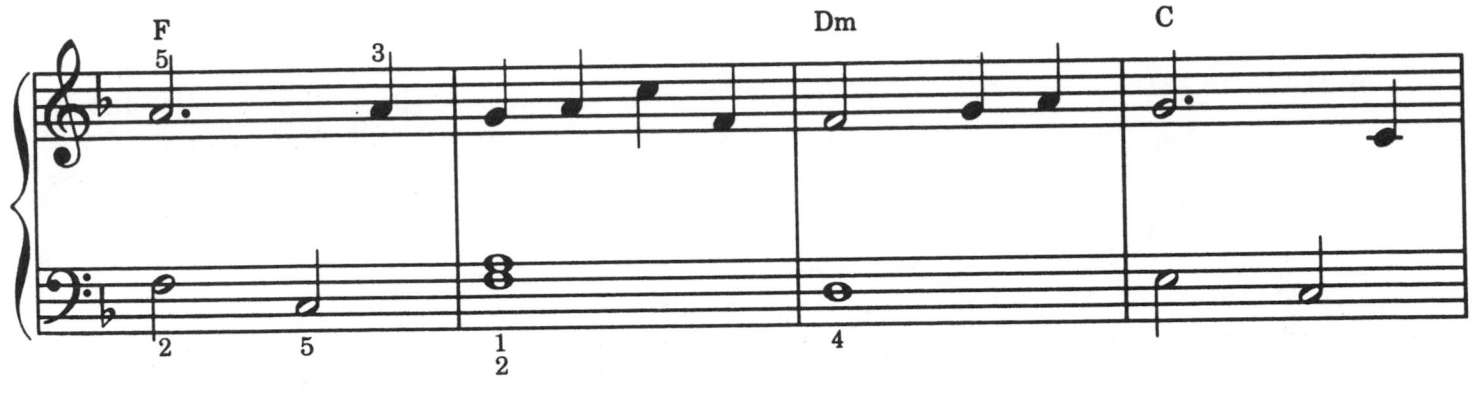

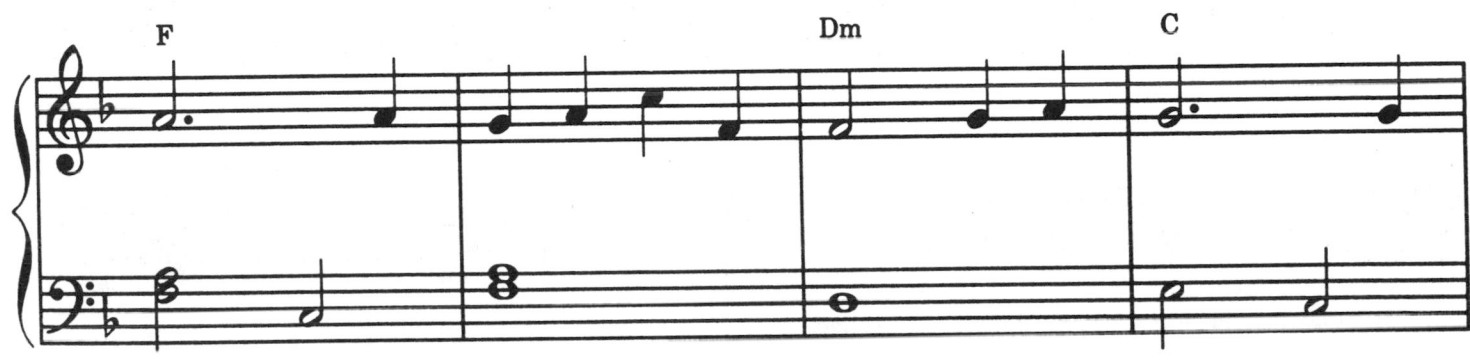

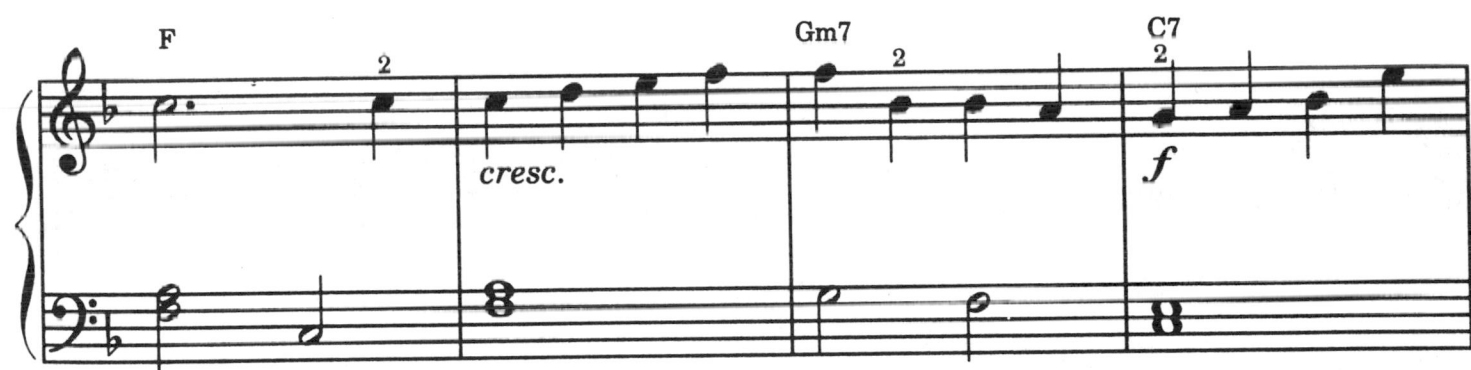

Do You Know The Way To San Jose?

Lyric by HAL DAVID

Music by BURT BACHARACH
Arr. by John W. Schaum, A.S.C.A.P.

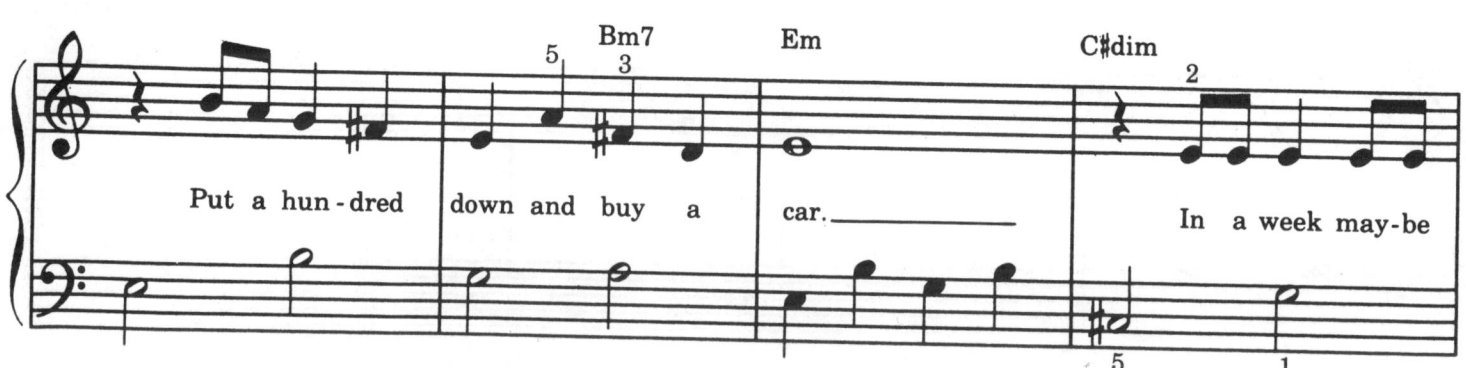

EL03368

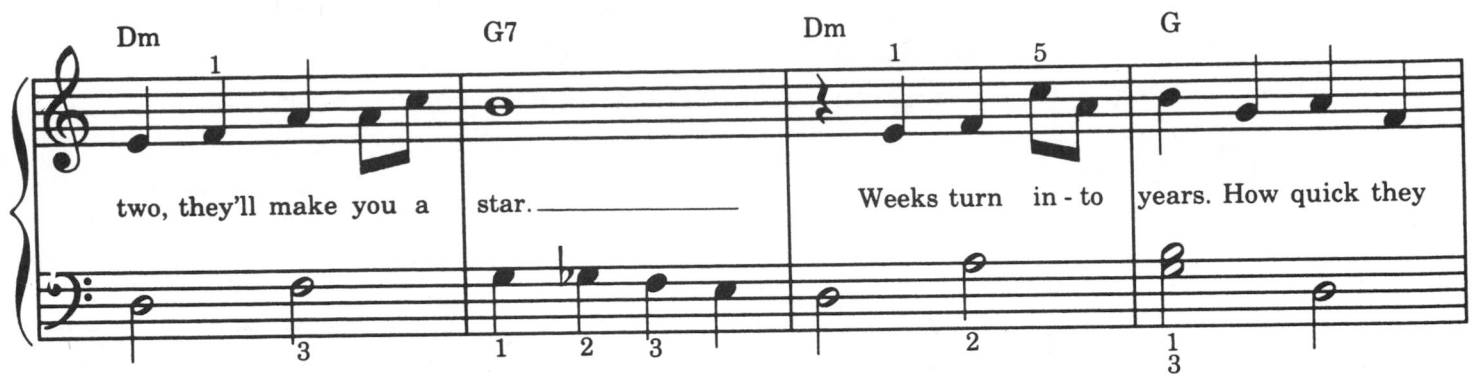

two, they'll make you a star._____ Weeks turn in-to years. How quick they

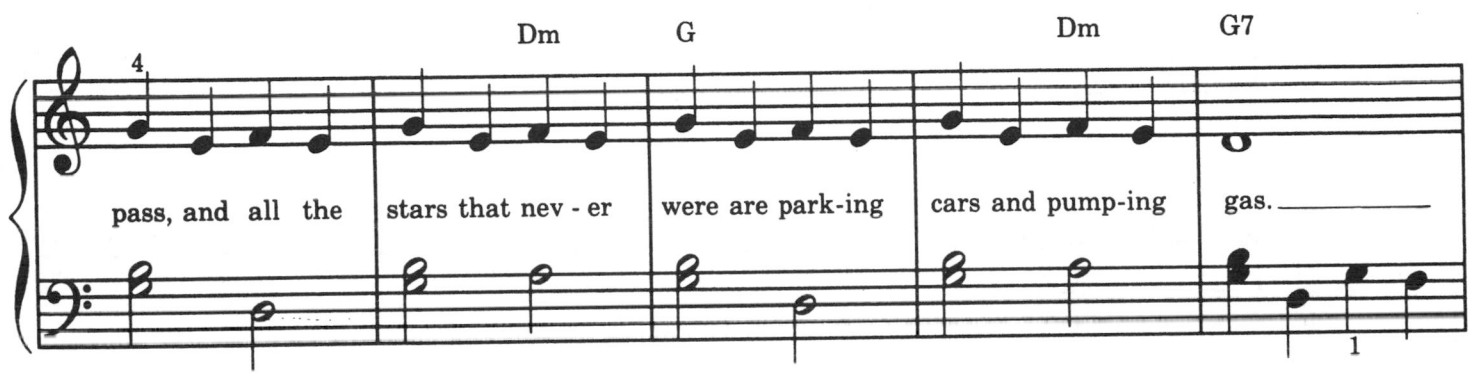

pass, and all the stars that nev-er were are park-ing cars and pump-ing gas._____

I've got lots of friends in San Jo-se. I'm on my way with-out an-y more de-lay.

Now I know the way to San Jo-se. That is the place I'll al-ways stay.

From The Paramount Picture "THE GODFATHER"

Speak Softly Love
(Love Theme From "The Godfather")

Words by LARRY KUSIK

Music by NINO ROTA
Arr. by Wesley Schaum

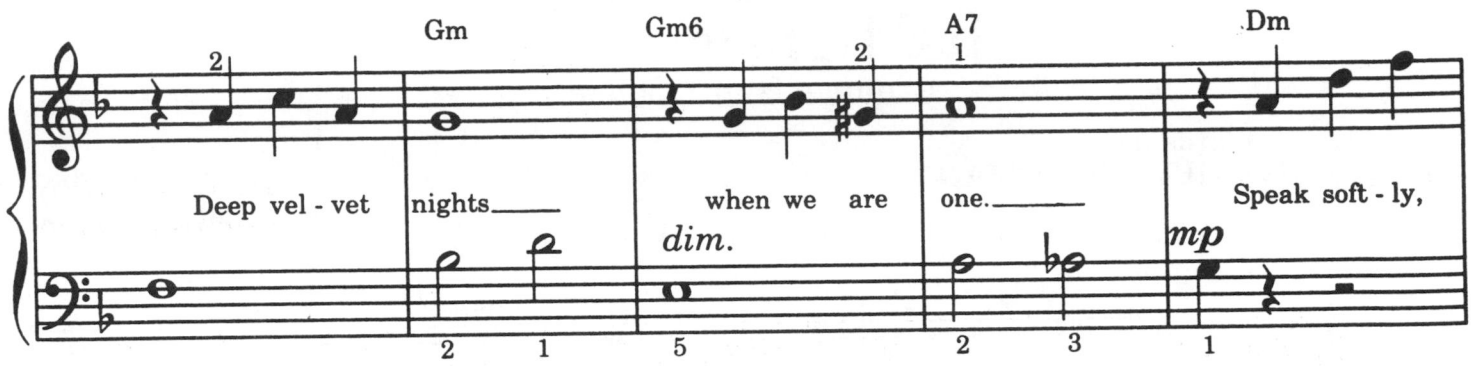

Deep vel - vet nights_____ when we are one._____ Speak soft - ly,

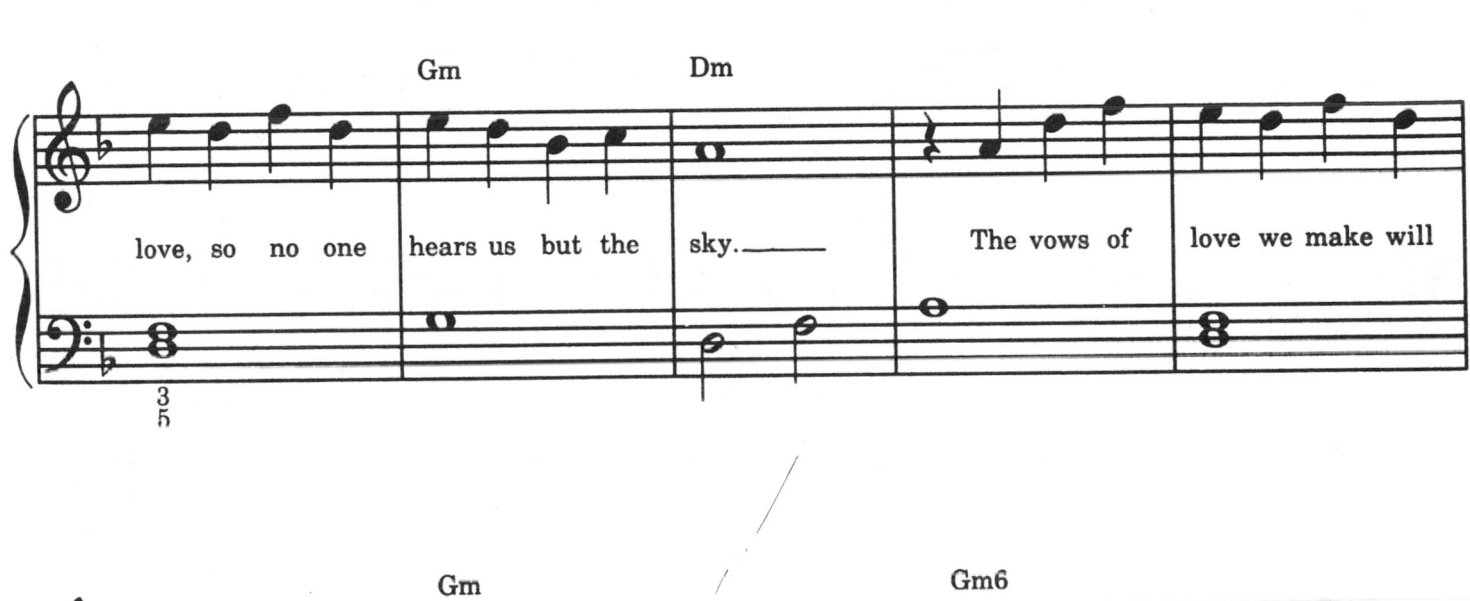

love, so no one hears us but the sky._____ The vows of love we make will

live un - til we die._____ My life is yours_____ and all be -

cause_____ You came in - to my world with love so soft - ly, love._____

COLUMBIA PICTURES Presents a MIRAGE/PUNCH Production a Sidney Pollack Film "TOOTSIE"

It Might Be You
(Theme from Tootsie)

Words by
ALAN and MARILYN BERGMAN

Music by
DAVE GRUSIN
Arr. by Wesley Schaum

EL03368

21

Blue Moon

Words by LORENZ HART

Music by RICHARD RODGERS
Arr. by Wesley Schaum

EL03368

The
BEST OF JOHN W. SCHAUM
Series

Favorite Schaum pieces available in convenient graded collections

Each book contains 23 compositions and arrangements for solo piano correlated with the John W. Schaum Piano Course books, levels Pre-A through D.

The Best of John W. Schaum:

—— (EL 03037)
Playable with the Pre-A Green Book

—— (EL 03038)
Playable with the A Red Book

—— (EL 03039)
Playable with the B Blue Book

—— (EL 03040)
Playable with the C Purple Book

—— (EL 03041)
Playable with the D Orange Book

The Christmas Book

—— (EL 03220)
A collection of compositions and arrangements of mixed grade levels, designed to span many years of study.